BLACK LIVES
MATTER

BY SUE BRADFORD EDWARDS AND DUCHESS HARRIS, JD, PHD

CONTENT CONSULTANT

Duchess Harris
Professor and Chair
American Studies Department
Macalester College

Essential Library

An Imprint of Abdo Publishing | abdopublishing.com

abdopublishing.com

Published by Abdo Publishing, a division of ABDO, PO Box 398166, Minneapolis, Minnesota 55439. Copyright © 2016 by Abdo Consulting Group, Inc. International copyrights reserved in all countries. No part of this book may be reproduced in any form without written permission from the publisher. Essential Library™ is a trademark and logo of Abdo Publishing.

Printed in the United States of America, North Mankato, Minnesota
082015
012016

Cover Photo: Andrew Burton/Getty Images
Interior Photos: Samuel Corum/Anadolu Agency/Getty Images, 6–7; St. Louis County Prosecutor's Office/Getty Images, 10; Robert Cohen/St. Louis Post-Dispatch/AP Images, 12; Cristina Fletes-Boutte/St. Louis Post-Dispatch/AP Images, 16; Hulton Archive/Getty Images, 18–19; Everett Historical/Shutterstock Images, 21; US Air Force, 25; AP Images, 27; US Government, 31; Justin Sullivan/Getty Images, 36–37, 54; Public Domain, 39; Douglas County Sheriff's Office/Getty Images, 41; Charles Steiner/Image Works/The LIFE Images Collection/Getty Images, 43; Ernest R. Prim/Shutterstock Images, 48–49; Saul Loeb/AFP/Getty Images, 51; Mario Tama/Getty Images, 56–57; Joe Burbank/Getty Images, 61; Marcus Yam/Los Angeles Times/Getty Images, 69; Frank Franklin II/AP Images, 71; Keith Srakocic/AP Images, 72–73; Rick Bowmer/AP Images, 75; Alex Brandon/AP Images, 77; Joshua Lott/Reuters/Newscom, 80–81; Ricardo Thomas/Detroit News/AP Images, 83; Clarence Tabb Jr./Detroit News/AP Images, 86; Carolyn Kaster/AP Images, 88–89; Patrick Record/The Ann Arbor News/AP Images, 93; Amy Davis/The Baltimore Sun/AP Images, 98

Editor: Arnold Ringstad
Series Designer: Maggie Villaume

Library of Congress Control Number: 2015944933

Cataloging-in-Publication Data
Edwards, Sue Bradford.
 Black lives matter / Sue Bradford Edwards and Duchess Harris.
   p. cm. -- (Special reports)
ISBN 978-1-62403-898-3 (lib. bdg.)
Includes bibliographical references and index.
1. African Americans--Social conditions--21st century--Juvenile literature. 2. Racism--United States--Juvenile literature.   3. Racial profiling in law enforcement--United States--Juvenile literature.   I. Title. II. Harris, Duchess, jt. author.
305--dc23

2015944933

CONTENTS

FOREWORD

#BlackLivesMatter is a call to action. It's a challenge to the criminal justice system. But most of all, it's a declaration of dignity. Yes, Black Lives Matter too.

The murder of Trayvon Martin and the acquittal of his killer George Zimmerman sparked the #BlackLivesMatter movement. Bold young leaders like Alicia Garza, Patrisse Cullors, and Opal Tometi coined the phrase. But it resonated for a reason. The nation witnessed it too many times: Harsh policing and sentencing for African Americans and impunity for vigilantes, like George Zimmerman, and police officers, like Darren Wilson.

#BlackLivesMatter resonated with me, a 51-year-old member of Congress. I vividly remember the acquittals of the police officers who brutalized Rodney King in 1991. After several of my own unpleasant interactions with police, the Rodney King acquittals left me feeling vulnerable, like my country had no regard for the lives of people like me. In that same year, I was a young activist and lawyer, and I remember sitting in the living room of Mrs. Earline Skinner, the mother of Tycel Nelson, 17, who was shot in the back by a police officer in north Minneapolis. Almost immediately, the press began to demonize him and lionize the officer. I remember this African-American mother telling me it seemed like her son's life "didn't matter." Through her tears, she resolved to seek justice for her dead child, and we filed suit and won a settlement which gave her some sense that someone besides her felt that her son's life did matter. When I heard Alicia Garza's call to action of #BlackLivesMatter, I felt it in my chest, and, for a moment, I was back in 1991.

When law enforcement officers shot and killed civil rights protester Jimmy Lee Jackson in Marion, Alabama, in 1965, he was seated in a diner with his mother and grandfather. The cop who shot him suspected he was peacefully challenging the Jim Crow status quo a few minutes earlier. Jimmy Lee Jackson was killed not for a legal violation but for defying the social norm of white supremacy in Alabama at that time. I suspect that the victims of police and vigilante violence today were also killed for violating a social norm too: being black and not deferential enough to white authority.

America has made unmistakable progress, but racially defined roles still exist. #BlackLivesMatter seeks to challenge them as a generation before it did. In 1965, the people took inspiration from Jimmy Lee Jackson's martyrdom and confronted Jim Crow again and again. They silently marched two-by-two across the Edmund Pettus Bridge, and were attacked by the Alabama state troopers and by vigilantes. Though many were injured on March 7, 1965, by the Alabama troopers, they did not quit. They were joined by allies and Dr. Martin Luther King. They eventually did march from Selma to Montgomery, and in August 1965 President Lyndon Johnson signed the Voting Rights Act of 1965 into law.

Jimmy Lee Jackson's death wasn't a moment in time, it sparked a movement. #BlackLivesMatter holds greater promise today, if we heed its call to action. It holds within it the possibility of a galvanizing, magnetic force. #BlackLivesMatter can do what Occupy Wall Street started but couldn't finish. It can unify and electrify a broad based movement which combines the disparate but parallel movements for a fair pay, student debt, immigration reform, a new union movement, and a resurgence in democratic participation. Such a movement is what this time calls for, and I believe #BlackLivesMatter has the charisma, vision, and organizational capacity to spark another major reordering of American social and economic relationships.

—CONGRESSMAN KEITH ELLISON, DISTRICT 5, MINNESOTA

CHAPTER ONE

MICHAEL BROWN AND FERGUSON

O n August 9, 2014, police officer Darren Wilson of Ferguson, Missouri, had just returned to his car when he heard the police dispatcher report a theft in progress. A young man was stealing cigars from a nearby convenience store. The dispatcher included a description of the man, and Wilson joined other officers who cruised the area looking for the suspect.

Wilson spotted Michael Brown and Dorian Johnson walking up the street. He drove toward them and stopped them because they were walking in the road. After Wilson stopped, he and Brown struggled through

The killing of Michael Brown in August 2014 triggered major protests about the issue of racial discrimination by police.

the window of the police sport-utility vehicle. Wilson's gun went off twice. Brown ran away, and Wilson exited the car and pursued Brown on foot. Brown turned and faced Wilson. The officer fired his gun, hitting Brown multiple times and killing him.

Wilson told investigators that Brown had tried to take his gun from him through the car's window. He said that when Brown ran, he got out of the vehicle and followed him, shooting Brown after Brown turned and confronted him.

Johnson told investigators Wilson pulled Brown through the window of the police sport-utility vehicle and fired a shot at him. He said Brown then held up his hands and tried to surrender, only to be shot down by Wilson.

HANDS UP, DON'T SHOOT

Dorian Johnson and 21 other witnesses said Brown's hands were up in surrender when Wilson shot him. Because of this, many later protesters held their hands over their heads, chanting "Hands up! Don't shoot!" Athletes made gestures in reference to the chant at sporting events. Students made posters with the slogan. But the physical evidence, including a bullet that passed through Brown's arm before entering his body, suggested Brown did not have his hands up in surrender when he was shot.

Some witnesses first said Wilson shot Brown in the back. Others said Brown was not moving toward Wilson. Many of these witnesses later contradicted themselves. Some later admitted they had not seen anything. They had repeated what other people said because they wanted to be part of a big story. Ten other witnesses gave accounts that agreed with the evidence. None saw Brown's hands up in surrender.

Other witnesses said Wilson had shot Brown in the back as he tried to flee. Investigators began working to piece together what really happened. As they tried to reconstruct the events of August 9, many people began forming opinions and taking sides on the shooting. Interest in the event spread through the city of Ferguson, the state of Missouri, and eventually the entire United States.

BROWN'S BODY

After the fatal shooting, Brown's body remained face down on the pavement where he had fallen. Parents who lived in nearby apartments made certain their children stayed in rooms facing away from the street. Adults came outside and took photos and videos as a stream of blood trickled from beneath Brown's head. People called their friends and local news stations to tell them what was happening.

Police draped a sheet over the body, but the sheet was too short. Brown's feet stuck out from the bottom, and his blood remained visible. By the time police blocked off the public's view of the body, photos and videos had already

Police and bystanders gathered around the scene of the shooting.

circulated through Twitter and Facebook. The images made their way to the national news.

As the hours passed, the crowd around the body grew angrier and louder. Some bystanders heard gunshots, though no one was hit and no shooters were found. When the driver contracted to transport bodies to the morgue for Saint Louis County arrived, he was not wearing a bulletproof vest. Police would not let him on the scene until things calmed down. By the time Brown's body was removed, he had been dead for four hours.

Sometimes a body remains at the scene of a death for hours because many people have jobs to do as part of the investigation of the death. What one person finds often determines what is done next. If Brown had been injured, a paramedic would have transported him to the hospital. Because the paramedic declared Brown dead, transporting the body became the responsibility of the county medical examiner. The shooting was a homicide, so Saint Louis County police took charge of the scene. This meant yet another wait. Although a four-hour wait is not unusual, crime scene experts believe a body should never be left in a public area for so long. People who saw Brown lying in the street for several hours felt the police were sending a message: this could be you.

THE REACTION

Many people did not believe justice would be done unless a public outcry forced the city government and police forces to fully investigate the shooting. The protests started out low-key. On August 10, the day after the shooting, the community held a vigil in memory of Brown. The protesters wanted the public to remember this young man as someone who mattered.

Late in the day, police officers, many wearing riot gear, attempted to disperse the crowd. People avoided the police. After dark, a few people smashed windows in cars and businesses and looted several stores.

Over the next several days, peaceful protests continued near the site of the shooting, near Ferguson

On August 10, local residents held a vigil outside the Ferguson police station.

police headquarters, and at the county police headquarters. Because of the looting, police asked people to protest only during daylight hours. On August 13, some protesters did not disperse at 9:00 p.m. Police used tear gas to break up the event. Reporters were also pushed back, and one news crew had tear gas thrown at them.

On August 14, the police tried a different tactic. State troopers marched alongside protesters. All remained peaceful until the next day, when the Ferguson police released a surveillance video of Brown robbing the convenience store in the hours before the shooting. Brown's family and other critics accused the police of trying to justify Wilson's use of force.

From that day through August 18, daylight protests remained peaceful, but riots broke out each night. At first, people threw rocks at police. When the police returned in armored trucks and teargassed the crowd, looters attacked businesses. Each night got progressively worse. Police patrolled in heavy trucks, wearing riot gear and using tear gas. Rioters threw makeshift firebombs. Multiple businesses were burned on August 18. The governor finally sent the National Guard into the area to restore peace.

On August 20, a grand jury started to review the evidence

FERGUSON AND THE CONSTITUTION

During the unrest in Ferguson, police arrested protesters and the reporters covering these events. Police also established a curfew to limit how late protests could be held. When protesters ignored the curfew, police fired on them with rubber bullets and tear gas.

The US Constitution guarantees citizens' rights even when they say things the government or police do not want to hear. In Ferguson, some argued that the police went against several of the Constitution's important provisions. They said the First Amendment, which guarantees freedom of speech and the right to meet peacefully, was violated when protesters and reporters were arrested.

"IF YOU ARE SUPPORTERS OF MICHAEL BROWN, YOU WILL HAVE FAITH AND KNOW JUSTICE WILL PREVAIL. STAY STRONG, RESIST IGNORANCE, AND DO NOT LET OFFICIALS PROVOKE YOU TO STEP OUTSIDE OF YOUR CHARACTER AND CREATE THE CHAOTIC ATMOSPHERE THEY EXPECT OF THE PEOPLE."[1]

—LOUIS HEAD, MICHAEL BROWN'S STEPFATHER

to decide if Officer Wilson would be charged with a crime. Peaceful protests continued, and people hoped justice would be done.

THE GRAND JURY'S DECISION

Interest in the grand jury's decision was high. On November 24, 2014, Saint Louis County Prosecuting Attorney Robert McCulloch announced the decision at a press conference on live television. Before revealing the jury's decision, he described how the Saint Louis County Police and the Federal Bureau of Investigation (FBI) had gathered evidence. He wanted people to know everything the jury knew, rather than focusing on one fact and using this single piece of information to decide what really happened. McCulloch said that because the public worried the investigation would favor the police department, he did not selectively decide what evidence to present to the Grand Jury, as is usually done. Instead, he presented them with every piece of evidence gathered.

McCulloch also talked about the problems with eyewitness testimony. He reminded viewers that many of the witness accounts were contradictory. Some bystanders claimed Wilson stood over Brown, who was lying face down, and shot Brown in the back. Other witnesses said Brown was shot in the back while running away. He pointed out that neither the county autopsy nor a second, private autopsy had found a gunshot wound in Brown's back.

Then McCulloch made the announcement. After meeting for three months, hearing more than 70 hours of testimony, and reviewing hundreds of photos, the jury decided no reason existed to indict Wilson.[2]

GRAND JURY DECISIONS

Grand juries work with a prosecuting attorney to see if there is enough evidence to take a case to trial. They review many different cases, but normally meet only a few days a month. This is part of the reason it can take so long for the public to find out whether there will be an indictment. It can take several weeks to get to a specific case.

The number of people on a grand jury ranges from 12 to 23. In Saint Louis County, the grand jury that reviewed the evidence against Darren Wilson consisted of 12 people. Nine of the jurors needed to agree for their decision to be final.[3]

Grand jury proceedings are secret; the jurors swear an oath not to reveal anything. The amount of information released about the grand jury for the Darren Wilson case was unusual.

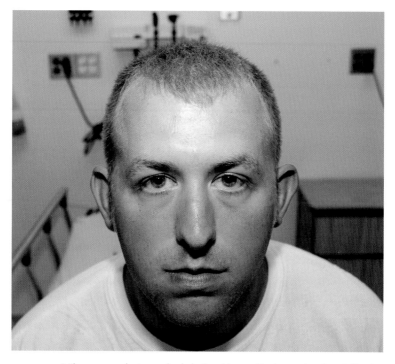
Wilson was photographed during his medical examination following the shooting.

Protesters, including Brown's mother and stepfather, had gathered in downtown Ferguson for the announcement. As soon as they heard there was no indictment, some protesters turned violent. They looted and burned businesses.

But Ferguson was not alone. In 170 cities throughout the United States, from New York to Los Angeles, California, people took to the streets.[4] They believed the authorities were treating the killing of Michael Brown as though it did not matter.

However, not all legal questions surrounding the events of August 9, 2014, had been settled. The US Department of Justice was carrying out its own investigation of Darren Wilson, the Ferguson Police Department, and the courts.

US Attorney General Eric Holder warned people that, although he had more than 40 FBI agents and civil rights prosecutors on the case, the investigation would take time. He emphasized that the government would support the rights of protesters, but he also said no violence would be tolerated while police worked to rebuild trust with the community.

BURN IT DOWN

The night the grand jury's findings were announced, Michael Brown's family waited in downtown Ferguson with a crowd of protesters. With the announcement that Wilson would not be charged, Louis Head, Brown's stepfather, comforted Brown's mother and then yelled out to the crowd to burn down the city.

Earlier in the day, Brown's family had asked everyone to protest peacefully, but their sorrow and anger boiled over. Head later told reporters this statement reflected his pain in the moment, but it was not what he wanted for his city.

"SOMETIMES THE WHEELS OF JUSTICE, PARTICULARLY IN CRIMINAL CASES, ARE SLOW. IT REQUIRES TIME TO COLLECT EVIDENCE. HAVING ANSWERS RIGHT AWAY MIGHT SATISFY YOUR CURIOSITY BUT THEY MAY NOT BE CORRECT. WE DON'T WANT TO INCARCERATE OR EVEN INDICT PEOPLE UNLESS WE'VE GOT THE EVIDENCE."[5]

—JUDY MELINEK,
FORENSIC PATHOLOGIST

CHAPTER TWO

BLACK LIVES
IN AMERICA

T he 1776 Declaration of Independence, one of the key founding documents of the United States, says "all men are created equal."[1] In reality, whites and African Americans have received unequal treatment throughout the nation's history. Many US whites of the 1700s and 1800s owned enslaved African Americans. Slaves were forced to work in harsh conditions for no pay. They picked cotton and performed other types of difficult physical labor. Their families were broken apart and sold. They were beaten or killed for resisting their enslavement.

When the new nation wrote the US Constitution, the basis for the structure of the

Many of the nation's founders, including George Washington, owned slaves.

US government and laws, in the 1780s, it made African Americans literally unequal. In an agreement known as the Three-Fifths Compromise, a slave would count as three-fifths of a person for the purposes of taxation and representation in the government. The agreement took place between the Northern states and the Southern states. In the North, slavery was on the road to being abolished. But in the South, slavery formed the basis of the regional economy. Millions of slaves worked on plantations, picking lucrative crops. The Three-Fifths Compromise limited the influence slave owners would have, preventing them from achieving additional representation in Congress as a result of their large slave populations.

These attitudes toward African Americans were reinforced in 1857 with a US Supreme Court case known as the Dred Scott decision. US Army Major John Emerson purchased Dred Scott, a slave, in 1832. When the army moved Emerson to Illinois, a free state, he brought Scott along. Scott married and started a family. Emerson later moved Scott to Missouri with his wife and daughter. When Emerson died, his widow rented Scott's labor to someone

The Dred Scott case made the unequal treatment of African Americans the law of the land.

else and kept his pay. When she would not let Scott buy his freedom, he took her to court because he had been living in free states for more than ten years. The US Supreme Court sided with Emerson's widow. Chief Justice Roger Taney said that the Declaration of Independence said all men are created equal, but enslaved Africans were not included because they had not helped write or sign this document. Scott remained a slave.

Tensions between the Northern states and the Southern states, driven largely by the slavery issue, eventually led to open conflict between the two sides in the American Civil War (1861–1865). Many Southern states seceded from the United States, forming the Confederate States of America. The Northern states, also known as the Union, fought to reunite the nation. In the midst of the war, on January 1, 1863, US president Abraham Lincoln issued the Emancipation Proclamation. This document declared all slaves living in the rebellious areas were free. Since the war was still underway, the proclamation had no real effect in the short term. Yet it made the end of slavery an explicit goal of the Union war effort.

POSTWAR DISCRIMINATION

The Union won the war in April 1865, but the victory did not result in instant equality between whites and African Americans. African Americans were no longer slaves, but they needed help adapting to their new lives. The US government created the Freedmen's Bureau, an organization that oversaw programs helping former slaves transition into their new lives as free citizens. Many farmed as sharecroppers, tenant farmers who paid their rent with a share of their crop. This left many former slaves extremely poor. Those who did not farm often held other menial jobs. Yet they did so as full citizens.

The Fifteenth Amendment to the US Constitution, ratified in 1870, made it illegal to keep any adult male from voting, regardless of his race or whether he had been a slave. It built on the foundation laid in 1868 by the Fourteenth Amendment, which called for all citizens to be equally protected by the law. Despite these amendments, many practices made it all but impossible for former slaves to vote in Southern states. Some polling locations charged taxes people could not afford to pay. Some officials demanded African Americans pass literacy tests, such as reciting the entire Constitution or explaining complicated laws, before they could vote. Even people with college degrees were turned away and told they could not vote.

In this social climate, segregation laws and customs separated African Americans from whites in everyday

THE FREEDMEN'S BUREAU

People who had lived their entire lives as slaves often lacked the skills and knowledge they needed to take their new places as free men and women. Because of this, the government established the Freedmen's Bureau in 1865. This federal agency helped people find food, places to live, and medical care. The bureau helped them find jobs and even enroll in school. Despite the good the bureau tried to do, a lack of funds and community hostility often hampered its efforts. It closed in 1872.

life. So-called Jim Crow laws kept African Americans in separate, substandard schools, prevented them from buying homes in white neighborhoods, and barred them from certain jobs.

WORLD WAR II

The situation improved marginally in the first decades of the 1900s. As the United States prepared to enter World War II (1939–1945), civil rights activist A. Philip Randolph told President Franklin D. Roosevelt there would be a massive protest in Washington, DC, if the president did not take action against racial discrimination. In response, Roosevelt issued an executive order that banned discrimination in war industries. However, the military itself remained segregated.

Though African Americans could join the military, they could not serve alongside white troops. Additionally, most were barred from combat duty, instead serving as cooks or in supply units. But some African Americans had the opportunity to serve in distinguished fighting units. Among these were the famous Tuskegee Airmen, fighter pilots who protected US bombers on missions deep into enemy territory. But even these elite units were segregated from white pilots and crews. Despite this treatment, they served with distinction.

THE CIVIL RIGHTS MOVEMENT

The success of segregated units demonstrated African Americans could excel in defense of their country. Yet US laws continued to treat them as second-class citizens. Frustrated people challenged these laws in the courts. For example, residents of several states filed lawsuits protesting the segregation of public schools. These lawsuits reached the US Supreme Court, where they

During World War II, African-American aviators showed themselves the equals of any other pilots.

became known collectively as *Brown v. Board of Education of Topeka*. In its 1954 decision on the case, the US Supreme Court outlawed segregated schools. The ruling served as a catalyst for additional change.

Sometimes change started with civil disobedience, or the refusal to obey an unjust law. One of the best-known examples of this occurred in Montgomery, Alabama. In Montgomery, African-American passengers sitting near the front of public buses were expected to give up their seats to white passengers and move to the back. On December 1, 1955, Rosa Parks refused to give up her seat to a white bus passenger. This action and her subsequent arrest led to the Montgomery Bus Boycott, a 381-day period when the African-American population of Montgomery refused to ride city buses.[2] People who walked rather than riding the bus were sometimes harassed and threatened.

BROWN V. BOARD OF EDUCATION OF TOPEKA

In its ruling in the case *Brown v. Board of Education of Topeka*, the US Supreme Court stated segregated schools are unconstitutional. The court also pointed out how segregation has a negative educational impact on African-American children. Sociologists and psychologists had done studies showing African-American children in segregated schools felt inferior to white children in similar schools. These negative feelings could affect their ability to learn.

Malcolm X was among the most controversial figures of the civil rights movement.

The boycotts were joined by other forms of protests. Protesting whites-only restaurants, African-American students sat peacefully at the lunch counters. Civil rights groups held leadership conferences as more and more people came together to work for equal rights. Some activists, such as Malcolm X, believed equality needed to be seized by any means. Others, such as Dr. Martin Luther King Jr., advocated for peaceful protests. Another activist, Ella Baker, worked with King to organize the Southern Christian Leadership Conference, an important civil rights group. She later left to work with the young people involved with the lunch counter sit-ins.

As the civil rights movement gained momentum, the resistance to it grew more violent. On May 4, 1961, a group of 13 activists began a bus trip from Washington, DC, through the South. They were the first of many activists known as the Freedom Riders. The African-American Freedom Riders activists attempted to use whites-only restrooms and eat at whites-only lunch

MALCOLM X

In 1952, Malcolm Little discarded his last name. He considered it a slave name, and he replaced it with X to symbolize the lost name of his ancestors. He joined the Nation of Islam, an African-American religious movement that called for African Americans to improve their standing in society. However, the group's extreme views, such as the idea of creating a separate country for African Americans, led critics to describe it as racist. Malcolm X told his followers in the group they needed to resist white aggression by any means necessary—even if it was not peaceful.

Malcolm X became an influential spokesperson for the Nation of Islam. The movement grew from roughly 400 members in 1952 to 40,000 members in 1960.[3] He encouraged young African Americans to take control of their lives. In the mid-1960s, Malcolm X left the Nation of Islam, joining a mainstream Muslim denomination and moderating his more extreme views. Members of the Nation of Islam assassinated him in 1965.

MORE TO THE
STORY

MARTIN LUTHER
KING JR.

Martin Luther King Jr. focused on ending legal segregation. After Rosa Parks was arrested for refusing to give up her bus seat, King led the Montgomery Bus Boycott and won a legal battle against the city. This confrontation brought him national attention.

King used nonviolent protest methods. He organized sit-ins at segregated lunch counters and peaceful demonstrations, including the 1963 March on Washington.

In 1964, the same year that the Civil Rights Act was passed, King received the Nobel Peace Prize. This award is given by a Norwegian committee to a person who has contributed significantly to peaceful causes. At 35, he became the youngest person at that time to receive this prestigious honor.

King continued to speak out for peace, organizing marches, disputing unfair housing practices, and protesting against US involvement in the Vietnam War (1955–1975). In April 1968, he was in Memphis, Tennessee, to support striking sanitation workers. On April 4, he was shot and killed while standing on his hotel balcony. He was 39 years old.

counters. The white riders did the reverse, making their way to the segregated facilities. In Anniston, Alabama, a mob of 200 angry whites surrounded the bus. When the driver refused to stop, the mob threw a bomb onto the bus. The riders escaped, but the US government was forced to send federal marshals to disperse the mobs.

Not every event was greeted with violence. On August 28, 1963, the March on Washington brought more than 200,000 people to peacefully protest in the plaza at the foot of the Lincoln Memorial.[4] It was at this event that King gave his famous "I Have a Dream" speech. Famed gospel singer Mahalia Jackson sang for the crowd.

In response to the widening civil rights movement, and more than 100 years after Lincoln's Emancipation Proclamation, the US government prepared to pass the Civil Rights Act of 1964. The legislation, designed to protect the freedoms of African Americans, threw federal support behind the idea that black lives matter.

"THIS CIVIL RIGHTS ACT IS A CHALLENGE TO ALL OF US TO GO TO WORK IN OUR COMMUNITIES AND OUR STATES, IN OUR HOMES AND IN OUR HEARTS, TO ELIMINATE THE LAST VESTIGES OF INJUSTICE IN OUR BELOVED COUNTRY."[5]

—LYNDON B. JOHNSON ON SIGNING THE CIVIL RIGHTS ACT

The March on Washington showcased the power of peaceful protests against injustice.

THE CIVIL RIGHTS ACT

In 1964, the Civil Rights Act expanded on the rights guaranteed by the Fourteenth and Fifteenth Amendments to the US Constitution. In addition to promises for equal treatment under law and the right to vote, the Civil Rights Act presented a detailed list of the types of discrimination the federal government would prohibit. With the passage of the Civil Rights Act, all state and local laws that legalized discrimination were overridden by the federal law.

The Civil Rights Act of 1964 made many types of discrimination illegal, including workplace discrimination. The law barred employers from discriminating against

THE EQUAL EMPLOYMENT OPPORTUNITY COMMISSION

The Equal Employment Opportunity Commission (EEOC) consists of five people appointed by the president who make sure the Civil Rights Act and related laws are enforced.

One of the jobs of the EEOC is to investigate individual complaints. A person who believes he or she has been subjected to discrimination because of race, age, religion, pregnancy, or national origin can file a report with the EEOC. The EEOC will also investigate whether someone has been discriminated against for the act of reporting discrimination.

But the EEOC does not just wait for complaints to be filed. It also requires employers to report on the race and gender of their employees. The EEOC reviews this information when looking for cases of discrimination based on lack of ethnic or gender diversity in a given workplace.

African-American job candidates due to their race. The act also meant labor unions had to support workers of all races, as well as women. If an employer was accused of discriminatory practices, the company could be investigated by the Equal Employment Opportunity Commission.

The act also made it illegal for public places to discriminate. There could no longer be segregated entrances to public buildings, such as courthouses. Whites-only parks, restaurants, hotels, and sports arenas became illegal. Separate seating in movie theaters was against the law. No program that received federal money could discriminate. This included school sports and aid packages, such as financial aid for attending a college or university.

Voting was also covered under the act. Whether the vote was for a local school board or the president of the United States, laws that allowed discriminatory practices for deciding who could register or cast a ballot became illegal. In 1965, the Voting Rights Act put additional measures in place to help keep this kind of discrimination from taking place.

A new law passed in 1968, the Fair Housing Act, prevented discrimination in the sale, rental, or financing of housing. It was the last major piece of legislation in the civil rights movement, but it had little impact on housing patterns. Between 1950 and 1980, the African-American urban population grew from 6.1 million to 15.3 million.[6] During this same time, a phenomenon known as white flight occurred. This was the movement of whites into suburban areas as African

VOTING RIGHTS ACT OF 1965

Equality is about more than jobs and homes. It is also about having a vote. On August 6, 1965, President Lyndon B. Johnson signed the Voting Rights Act into law.

This law was designed to overcome state and local barriers to African-American voters. It banned all poll taxes and provided for federal oversight of voter registration in areas where significant portions of the African-American population had not registered to vote. Federal officers could also monitor individual polling places when the time came for African-American voters to cast their ballots.

Americans began living in the inner cities. Whites often took job opportunities with them, contributing to unemployment in the cities.

IDENTIFYING THE GAPS

Public places could no longer discriminate, but private clubs could. This meant private pools, swimming clubs, golf courses, and similar organizations could continue using race as a determining factor when deciding who could join. African-American women, gays, and lesbians often faced additional discrimination.

There were also size limits in terms of housing and business. Businesses with 15 or fewer employees were exempt from proving they do not discriminate. So were boarding

THE COMBAHEE RIVER COLLECTIVE

An African-American feminist lesbian group known as the Combahee River Collective, active in the 1970s, addressed the problems of sexual exploitation and oppression experienced by African-American women. Among their causes was the support of Kenneth Edelin, an African-American doctor in Boston who was charged with manslaughter after performing a legal abortion. They also supported Ella Ellison, an African-American woman accused of murder simply because she was seen in the area where a person had been killed.

In 1977, the collective wrote the "Combahee River Collective Statement," a document that discussed sexual discrimination in the African-American community as well as racial discrimination in the larger feminist movement. This statement formed the groundwork for many feminists of color who organized later movements in the 1980s and the 1990s.

houses, apartments, and other types of housing with three or fewer units.

Those who framed the law may have felt small business and housing developments were inconsequential. Unfortunately, the numbers add up even in modern times. In the 2010s, businesses with 15 or fewer workers employed 16 percent of the US labor force—a total of approximately 19 million people. The exemptions in housing affected 20 percent of the housing market.[7]

Gaps in the Civil Rights Act allow some racist behaviors to continue. But unequal treatment is not limited to housing and employment. Despite the promise of equal protection under the law for all Americans, serious examples of inequality occur in the US legal system. Often, these problems begin with the differing treatment of whites and African Americans by police forces.

CHAPTER THREE

OSCAR
GRANT

O n New Year's Day 2009, police with Bay Area Rapid Transit (BART), the rail service that runs through San Francisco and Oakland, California, responded to reports of a fight. Seven officers reported to the Fruitvale BART station in Oakland, where they ordered 22-year-old Oscar Grant and several other men off the train.

Passengers at the station recorded the incident using their smartphone cameras. Video footage of the event shows Grant struggling briefly with two of the officers, including Johannes Mehserle, before he is subdued. At that point, Grant lay face down on the platform. An officer had his knee on Grant's head and neck. Both of Grant's hands were behind his back.

The killing of Oscar Grant in January 2009 was captured on video.

Mehserle told the second officer to move clear. He pulled out his gun and shot Grant in the back. Grant had been unarmed. He was taken to a nearby hospital, where he died the following morning.

PROTESTS TURN VIOLENT

On January 7, following Grant's funeral, approximately 500 protesters gathered at the BART station where Grant had been killed. From the station, the crowd marched through Oakland's business district, where Oakland police officers blocked roads and attempted to disperse the crowd.

The protesters surrounded a police car with an officer in it. Other police forces approached the group from behind and fired tear gas into the crowd in an attempt to break up the protest.

The Fruitvale BART station became the focus of nationwide attention following the events of January 1, 2009.

The group did not disperse but instead moved elsewhere. Some of them blocked intersections, lying face down on the pavement, mimicking Grant's position when he was shot. Protesters carried signs reading "Your Idea of Justice?" and "Jail Killer Cops."[1] Protesters also lit candles in memory of Grant.

Again, police attempted to break up the protest. This time they wore helmets and gas masks, and they formed standing lines to channel the protest away from the station. An hour later, when the crowd had not dispersed, police gave the order to fire rubber bullets and more tear gas. As the protesters moved down the street, some threw rocks and bottles at the police. Police helicopters shone spotlights onto the street.

Some of the protesters began rioting, setting fire to trash cans, dumpsters, and cars. Windshields and storefront windows were smashed. Over the course of the night, more than 100 people were arrested.[2]

Oakland mayor Ron Dellums condemned the destruction, but he said he understood the cause and recognized people's frustrations. Citizens had clearly lost faith in the police authorities, in part because the BART police had been so silent about the investigation they had begun into the shooting. He encouraged people to stay hopeful.

AGITATORS

When the post-trial protests gave way to riots, Oakland officials said these people were not local residents and protesters but agitators from the outside. Three out of every four people arrested were not from Oakland. Some of these rioters carried Molotov cocktails, improvised firebombs made up of flammable liquid in a glass bottle. Others used baseball bats. Their violent actions tainted some people's view of the protests, even though there were also many peaceful protesters from Oakland.

Mehserle was arrested 12 days after the shooting.

THE TRIAL

The prosecuting attorney's office decided to try Mehserle for murder. People hoped this might set a precedent for police officers being held accountable for excessive force, since there was no previous case of a California police officer being tried for murder for an on-duty killing. For this case, there was evidence from witness interviews and video evidence from smartphones.

FROM THE
HEADLINES

RODNEY KING AND THE LOS ANGELES RIOTS

The shooting of Oscar Grant was another in a long line of police incidents captured on video by a bystander. Among the earliest instances of this came in 1991 and centered around Los Angeles resident Rodney King.

On March 3, 1991, police pursued Rodney King in a high-speed chase through Los Angeles, California. When they pulled him over, they dragged him out of the car and beat him severely. Bystander George Holliday captured the beating on videotape from the window of his apartment.

Holliday contacted the police department to offer them the tape. When the police did not respond, he turned the tape over to a local news station. Long before the advent of social media and YouTube, the video aired on one news station after another, spreading across the United States.

The four officers who took part in the beating were charged with assault with a deadly weapon and excessive use of force. Despite the video and King's injuries, a jury acquitted the officers of these charges.

Holliday's video showed the police officers repeatedly striking King with batons.

The public rage that followed sparked the 1992 Los Angeles riots. The violence continued for six days, though the worst of it occurred in the first two days. More than 50 people were killed, more than 2,000 were injured, and approximately 9,500 people were arrested for rioting.[3] The destruction added up to $1 billion in property damage.[4] The arrival of the California Army National Guard and a dusk-to-dawn curfew ended the violence.

During the trial, Mehserle testified he saw Grant reaching toward his pocket and feared Grant had a hidden gun. He stated he had meant to stun Grant, intending to draw his Taser but accidentally pulling out his pistol. Some experts who viewed the video evidence say they saw him hesitate before drawing his gun, showing that perhaps he was confused and meant to draw his Taser.

After deliberating for more than six hours over a two-day period, the jury found Mehserle guilty of the charge of manslaughter, rather than murder. This meant that though video evidence and witness testimonies may have shown excessive force, the jury did not believe Mehserle had meant to kill Grant.

THE REACTION

After the verdict was announced, the prosecuting

FRUITVALE STATION

Fruitvale Station, a movie made by writer and director Ryan Coogler, tells the story of the last day of Oscar Grant's life. Some critics claim the movie plays with the facts and tries to make Grant into a better person than he was. Others say the writing and acting clearly show Grant's flaws.

When Coogler watched the trial, he noticed something. "Oscar was either cast as a saint who had never done anything wrong in his life, or he was painted as a monster who got what he deserved that night," Coogler said.[5] Coogler said his goal in making the film was to show both the good and the bad in Grant, portraying him as a real human being.

attorney spoke to the press. "We believe Johannes Mehserle was guilty of the crime of murder," she said. "We presented the case that way, we presented the evidence that way, and the jury found otherwise."[6]

Many people shared her belief. A crowd of approximately 500 protesters marched through Oakland. Although the initial protest was peaceful, as night fell, some protesters began rioting, burning, and looting. That night, the police arrested 83 people for damaging shops and cars as well as setting fires.[7]

Despite these arrests, the local police chief praised the protest organizers. Working with city officials, most of the protesters had taken part in a peaceful event. The police also made an effort to maintain the peace. Rather than confronting protesters carrying rocks and bottles, they gave them space. Though a few protesters had chosen violence, less damage occurred than during the pretrial riots.

Mehserle's criminal trial was not the end of the investigation into Oscar Grant's death. Even before the end of the criminal trial, the federal government had been approached to investigate Grant's death and to see if there was enough evidence for a federal lawsuit.

After the criminal verdict was read, the federal government announced it was investigating whether Grant's civil rights had been violated. In the end, the federal jury decided there had been no civil rights violations.

In July 2010, Mehserle was sentenced to two years in jail. As a result of good behavior and California's prison overcrowding, he was released after serving approximately one year. The fact remained that a young African-American man who posed no immediate threat had been shot and killed. The sentence for the killer, whether the act was intentional or unintentional, struck many people as extremely light. For many, the case highlighted that

DOUBLE JEOPARDY?

The Fifth Amendment to the US Constitution prohibits double jeopardy, or being tried twice for the same crime. How then could Johannes Mehserle be tried and convicted of manslaughter in the killing of Oscar Grant and then face additional federal charges for the same crime?

This happens when different government departments have overlapping jurisdictions. This means both departments have authority over a particular area. The local police had authority over the crime, while federal law enforcement had authority over civil rights issues. Because of this, Mehserle could be tried for Grant's death and for violating the civil rights of his family. The charges were not the same, though they centered on the same event.

equality had not been achieved. Civil rights activists and others renewed their efforts to work for justice.

"THIS IS WHERE WE, AS PARENTS, HAVE TO BE RELENTLESS IN THE VINDICATION OF OUR SLAIN SONS. THROUGH OUR PAIN AND FRUSTRATION, WE MUST SHAKE THE CONSCIOUSNESS OF AMERICA AND MAKE SOCIETY ANSWER WHY IT EMPOWERS LAW ENFORCEMENT TO KILL OUR UNARMED CHILDREN."[8]

—**WANDA JOHNSON, MOTHER OF OSCAR GRANT**

CHAPTER FOUR

UNEQUAL
JUSTICE

B efore the civil rights movement, laws provided differing punishments for white and African-American offenders. These punishments were consistently harsher for African Americans. Such laws no longer exist, but the underlying attitudes linger, frequently leading to unequal treatment by law enforcement and the criminal justice system.

One of the reasons the US Justice Department began looking so closely at civil rights issues in Ferguson is because of the unbalanced statistics of the city's law enforcement system. In 2013, the Ferguson courts issued 32,975 arrest warrants, an average of more than one for each of the city's 21,135 people.[1] The vast majority of these warrants were issued for traffic

Statistics show law enforcement in the United States often targets African Americans disproportionately, including in traffic stops.

violations. Though African Americans made up 67 percent of the city's overall population, 86 percent of the drivers stopped by the police were black.[2] Drivers who are pulled over for speeding, rolling through a stop sign, or failing to signal a turn have to pay a fine for the violation plus a court fee. When these drivers cannot afford pay, a warrant is issued for their arrest.

INJUSTICE BY THE NUMBERS

- African-American males are six times as likely to be killed by police as white males.
- One-third of all African-American males will spend time behind bars.
- One-third of African-American males in their twenties are currently under the control of the justice system because they are in prison or jail or on probation or parole.
- One-tenth of African-American males in their twenties are incarcerated.[3]

Ferguson is not the only place where police have a history of disproportionally stopping African-American drivers. US Justice Department statistics for 2011 for the nation as a whole showed an African-American driver was 31 percent more likely to be pulled over than a white driver. Approximately 5 percent of African-American drivers were not told why they were pulled over, nearly double the rate among whites. Once stopped, African-American drivers were more than twice as likely to be subjected to a vehicle search.[4]

THE WAR ON DRUGS

African Americans receive harsher treatment not only at the hands of law enforcement, but also within the court system. This is especially evident in relation to the war on drugs, the US effort to reduce the illegal drug trade. Though the United States no longer has separate legal penalties for African Americans and whites, prosecuting attorneys have a great deal of leeway in charging individual defendants.

An example of this form of inequality can be seen in the cases of Richard Thomas and Tim Carter. Both were

Many activists argue the war on drugs leads to discriminatory policies against African Americans and should be replaced with a new drug policy.

arrested in the same part of Saint Petersburg, Florida, in 2004. The arrests came a few months apart. Carter, who is white, was arrested in possession of the illegal drug cocaine. He identified himself as a drug addict but had no arrests or convictions. Thomas, who is African-American, was arrested carrying a crack pipe that had some residue of crack, another form of cocaine. Like Carter, Thomas said he was an addict. He had no prior arrests or convictions.

Both men faced a maximum sentence of five years. Carter was not tried. Instead, he was sent by the judge to a drug rehabilitation program. Thomas, on the other hand, was tried, convicted, and sent to prison. The only major difference between these two men was race, yet they received radically different treatment within the criminal justice system.

Some people assume more African Americans receive harsher penalties because crack cocaine use is more common among African-American drug users than white drug users. At one time this was true. In 2000, 80 percent of crack offenders were African Americans, while less than 6 percent were white. But by 2006, 65 percent of crack cocaine addicts were white. Still, ten African Americans were charged for possession for each white defendant charged.[5]

Inner-city gang warfare accompanied crack cocaine sales. Drug-selling gangs fought to control larger areas and thus a larger number of users. Civic organizations in these mostly African-American neighborhoods wanted to reduce crime, so they pushed for and received harsher penalties. The difference between penalties for cocaine powder and crack cocaine may have stemmed from this effort. Still, the result has been harsher penalties for African Americans, even for similar crimes.

DOING TIME

When the war on drugs began in the 1970s, there were 300,000 inmates in US prisons. The US prison population in the 2010s, including those in private prisons, is approximately 2 million.[6] More than half are convicted of drug-related crimes. The United States has

PRIVATE PRISONS

Not only does the United States have more prisoners than ever before, many of them are held in private prisons. A private prison is designed to make money rather than rehabilitate inmates. The prisons earn money on each inmate they house. Their contracts with the government require them to maintain certain occupancy rates. If they do not, taxpayers are charged for the empty beds. Critics say that because of this, the courts have an incentive to continue sending a certain number of people to prison.

Prison overcrowding in California has led to the conversion of gyms and other common spaces into prisoner housing areas.

the largest prison population of any country in the world. Three-quarters of those imprisoned for drug offenses are African-American or Latino.[7]

African Americans are incarcerated at more than five times the rate of whites.[8] In addition, they receive longer sentences. A 2000 study found that African Americans in the Kansas City, Missouri, area who were convicted of drug-related crimes received sentences 14 months longer than those received by whites.[9] No similar racial disparity existed in the sentences given out for violent crimes.

The problem is not just that African Americans receive more and longer prison sentences. It is also the effects these prison sentences have on the lives of individuals and families. Prisoners cannot earn incomes to help support spouses, children, or parents. Their absences create financial and emotional burdens on their families and their communities, creating economically and educationally depressed neighborhoods. This may leave children living in these areas behind their peers from the start. It may be incredibly difficult for them to catch up.

There is another long-lasting impact of this high rate of imprisonment: prison inmates often permanently lose the right to vote. Very few states allow convicts or ex-convicts to vote. Still, the census counts prisoners when tallying representation in the districts in which they temporarily reside. The result is that though a higher number of prisoners are black, many prisons are located in largely white areas, meaning these white areas have increased representation while the poorer areas where ex-inmates live have decreased representation.

CRADLE-TO-PRISON PIPELINE

The term *cradle-to-prison pipeline* has been used to describe the complex web of economic, social, and political factors that seem to lead many poor African-American children straight into the prison system. In her best-selling book, *The New Jim Crow*, Michelle Alexander explains there are more African Americans in the correctional system today than were enslaved in 1850. What are the elements that feed into this? Marian Wright Edelman, president of the Children's Defense Fund, says they include poverty, unequal access to health and mental health care, low-quality schools, and a malfunctioning child welfare system. To interrupt the pipeline, her organization argues adults must have jobs with a livable wage, schools must be improved, people must receive access to affordable health care, and there must be programs in place to help young people to turn their lives around.

CHAPTER FIVE

TRAYVON
MARTIN

On the evening of February 26, 2012, 17-year-old Trayvon Martin walked through a neighborhood in Sanford, Florida. It was raining, and he was talking on his cell phone with a friend. He had been to a local store to buy snacks for himself and another friend, and he was returning to his father's fiancée's home.

Before he reached home, he was spotted by 28-year-old George Zimmerman, who was driving through the gated community. Zimmerman was not a police officer. Instead, he was a member of a neighborhood watch group that patrolled the area to report potential crimes to the police. When he saw Martin, he became suspicious of the hoodie-wearing teen. He called 911.

The killing of Trayvon Martin drew attention to the issues of profiling and self-defense laws.

"This guy looks like he's up to no good or he's on drugs or something," Zimmerman said to the emergency dispatcher. "It's raining, and he's just walking around looking about. . . . He's got his hand in his waistband. And he's a black male. . . . Something's wrong with him. Yup, he's coming to check me out. He's got something in his hands."[1]

There had been numerous recent robberies in the community. This may have contributed to Zimmerman's suspicions. The dispatcher told him to remain in his car and not to follow Martin. Zimmerman ignored this request.

Martin noticed he was being followed. He told his friend on the phone about Zimmerman. The friend was frightened for Martin. She listened from the other end of the line as Zimmerman asked Martin what was going on. Then the call disconnected.

Several moments later, Zimmerman and Martin were struggling on the ground. Witnesses heard one of them call for help before a single gunshot was fired. When police arrived on the scene, Martin lay dead on the pavement.

THE TRIAL

Initially, the police did not file any charges against Zimmerman. According to the local police chief, they had no reason to doubt Zimmerman's version of events. He claimed he was attacked and had to fight back. His facial injuries seemed to support the fact that he had been injured in a struggle. With no definitive evidence

"THERE ARE EVENTS LIKE THIS THAT HIGHLIGHT AND EMPHASIZE THE FACT THAT WE STILL HAVE A LONG WAY TO GO. WE CANNOT BE COMPLACENT IN OUR SOCIETY WHEN WE STILL HAVE A DRAMATIC DISPARITY BETWEEN BLACK YOUTH UNEMPLOYMENT AND NON-BLACK YOUTH UNEMPLOYMENT."[2]

—ARIZONA SENATOR JOHN MCCAIN ON THE SHOOTING OF TRAYVON MARTIN

MILLION HOODIE MARCH

In Manhattan, New York, on March 21, 2013, protesters marched in the Million Hoodie March, calling out "We want arrests."[3] Many marchers wore hooded sweatshirts to focus on the importance that profiling played in the death of Trayvon Martin.

Martin's parents happened to be in New York at the time of the march. They spoke with protest leaders and promised they would continue to demand justice. Sybrina Fulton, Martin's mother, said, "My heart is in pain, but to see the support of all of you really makes a difference."[4]

Zimmerman had not acted in self-defense, the police had no plans to make an arrest.

Martin's family could not accept that their son's killer wouldn't face justice. His parents posted an online petition demanding Zimmerman be arrested and tried. By then, the story of Martin's death had become national news. More than 2.25 million people signed the petition.[5]

As the number of signatures on the petition grew, people in Florida let their opinions be known. A few weeks after Martin's death, students in 34 Miami schools walked out of class, demanding justice.[6] There was also a protest in Sanford. In an attempt to calm the public, the Sanford City Commission organized a town hall meeting about the incident and invited Martin's parents to speak.

Many people believed Zimmerman targeted Martin because he was black. Officials finally bowed to public pressure. On April 11, 2012, Zimmerman

PROFILING PROBLEMS

In racial profiling, a person is suspected of a crime or other wrongdoing based on race, ethnicity, appearance, or other factors. These suspicions are often based on stereotypes. Typically, the term *racial profiling* is used to describe such discrimination by law enforcement officials. When Zimmerman saw Martin and thought he was acting suspiciously, the hoodie-wearing 17-year-old was a victim of similar profiling.

During the trial, Zimmerman's defense attorneys presented images of his injuries to suggest their client had acted in self-defense.

was arrested and charged with second-degree murder, meaning he knew his action would kill Martin but did not plan the killing ahead of time.

Throughout the trial, the jurors were presented with a wide assortment of evidence. Zimmerman testified he lay on the ground as Martin sat atop his chest, beating Zimmerman's head into the concrete. Zimmerman also testified his holstered gun was in plain sight, and he said Martin reached for it. Zimmerman stated he beat Martin to the firearm and shot the 17-year-old in the

MORE TO THE
STORY

STAND YOUR GROUND

In 2005, Florida governor Jeb Bush signed a broad self-defense law
called the stand-your-ground law. The law enables Florida residents
to kill an intruder or attacker in order to defend themselves. The law
does not require that the person under attack attempt to flee.

When a person who is on trial uses this law in his or her
defense, the defendant does not have to prove he or she was in
danger of being killed. The person only has to show that resorting
to force would have seemed reasonable. The burden of proof is on
the prosecuting attorney, who has to prove the person on trial did
not act in self-defense but was on the attack.

Zimmerman's lawyer, Mark O'Mara, did not rely on the
stand-your-ground law. He did not feel he had time to prepare
for a stand-your-ground hearing, which would have to take place
before the trial itself. Still, after the trial, people called for changes
to stand-your-ground laws, believing they encouraged shootings of
African Americans without consequences.

chest. Once Zimmerman's testimony, testimonies from various witnesses, forensic evidence, and photos of Zimmerman's injuries had been presented, it was up to the jury to determine what had really happened on that rainy February evening.

THE ACQUITTAL

After hearing the evidence, the jury had three choices: they could find Zimmerman guilty of second-degree murder; they could find him guilty of a lesser charge of manslaughter; or they could find him not guilty. To find him guilty of second-degree murder, the jurors would have to believe Zimmerman knew what he did would kill Martin. To find Zimmerman guilty of manslaughter, the jurors would have to believe he meant to do what he did and that, though his actions led to Martin's death, he did not hate Martin or intend to kill him.

"LET TRAYVON'S DEATH NOT BE FOR NAUGHT. LET US HONOR HIS LIFE BY RIGHTING THIS WRONG, AND SEEING THAT JUSTICE IS SERVED FOR TRAYVON AND HIS FAMILY. GEORGE ZIMMERMAN MUST BE PROSECUTED FOR HIS ADMITTED SHOOTING OF TRAYVON MARTIN AND THE 'STAND YOUR GROUND' LAW MUST BE REPEALED."[7]

— CONGRESSMAN ALCEE HASTINGS, DISTRICT 20, FLORIDA

To many, Zimmerman's testimony did not seem to add up. In the courtroom, he testified he had been on the ground with Martin sitting on his chest. He also testified his gun was holstered and visible. But Zimmerman's claim about the gun would not have been possible with Zimmerman lying on his back. Following the killing of Martin, the police took Zimmerman back to the crime scene and videotaped him walking them through the events that led to the shooting. Three different times in the video, Zimmerman can be seen and heard telling the police his gun was holstered in the small of his back. This means it would have been pressed to the ground and invisible if he had been on his back with Martin sitting on him.

The prosecuting attorney had access to all of this information and should have been able to refute

RACHEL JEANTEL

When Zimmerman encountered Martin, Martin was on the phone with Rachel Jeantel. When called to testify in Zimmerman's trial, she became a controversial witness not because of what she said but because of how she said it.

Courtrooms are a space with well-defined rules concerning respect and how a question should be answered. Jeantel did not conform to these expectations. Some saw her attitude in court as dismissive, aggressive, or hostile. At the same time, others believed she was being candid and authentic.

Zimmerman's testimony. Critics assert the police and the prosecuting attorney's office had not wanted to arrest Zimmerman and were willing to believe his version of events. Nothing in the public outcry that forced the arrest had changed their minds. The prosecution failed to refute Zimmerman's testimony, leading the jury to believe he did not intentionally kill Martin. On July 13, 2013, the jury found Zimmerman not guilty.

THE REACTION

The public had been following the case closely, and reactions to the verdict were varied. In the United States, many people focused on race. Many African Americans felt Martin would still be alive if he had not been black. Some whites agreed, but others were satisfied with Zimmerman's acquittal. A poll taken by ABC News and the *Washington Post* showed 86 percent of African-American respondents

"ACROSS AMERICA, DIVERSE GROUPS OF CITIZENS, FROM ALL RACES, BACKGROUNDS, AND WALKS OF LIFE, ARE . . . OVERWHELMINGLY MAKING THEIR VOICES HEARD—AS AMERICAN CITIZENS HAVE THE RIGHT TO DO—THROUGH PEACEFUL PROTESTS, RALLIES, AND VIGILS DESIGNED TO INSPIRE RESPONSIBLE DEBATE."[8]

—ERIC HOLDER, US ATTORNEY GENERAL

were unhappy with the verdict, while only 30 percent of white respondents were dissatisfied.[9]

From coast to coast, Americans who were unhappy with the verdict raised their voices in protest. On Monday, July 14, 2013, hundreds of New Yorkers marched into Times Square. Marchers also took to the streets in San Francisco, California. On Tuesday, protesters marched in Houston, Texas, and Atlanta, Georgia.

Following the acquittal, many people raised their voices on social media. On Twitter alone, nearly 5 million tweets circulated in the 26 hours after the verdict was announced. Those angered by the acquittal outnumbered those who supported it by a ratio of 4 to 1.[10]

When Zimmerman was acquitted, the Black Youth Project was meeting in Chicago, Illinois. This activist organization gathers information about what is going on in the lives of African-American youth; it teaches these youth how to use politics and public awareness to make changes in their communities. One hundred young activists had gathered to decide how to take their organization beyond electoral politics. They needed a plan for what else they could do that would improve lives in their communities. When they heard Zimmerman had been acquitted, they knew they had to do something. Part of the group left the meeting and led a rally in downtown Chicago, while other delegates stayed behind and drafted a public letter to the family of Trayvon Martin and African Americans everywhere.

As the Black Youth Project drafted their letter and led the rally, other people around the country expressed their outrage about Zimmerman's acquittal on Facebook and Twitter. An activist named Patrisse Cullors started using the Twitter hashtag #BlackLivesMatter to focus attention not just on the killing of African Americans, but also on the fact that these people and their lives mattered. In just a few days,

OBAMA'S PRESS CONFERENCE

On July 19, 2013, President Obama held a press conference to encourage Americans to take five constructive steps following Zimmerman's acquittal. He first suggested that the Justice Department and local governments work with police departments to examine the ways they might be biased against the populations they serve. Secondly, he encouraged communities to look at laws, such as stand-your-ground laws, that help create confrontation instead of defusing it. Third, he asked communities to encourage young African-American boys to succeed in school and in life. Fourth, he said people need to discuss race with others in their communities. Finally, he encouraged people to have hope and remember that, slow as progress may seem, things are getting better.

MORE TO THE STORY

THE ORIGINS OF BLACK LIVES MATTER

Alicia Garza created Black Lives Matter with Patrisse Cullors and Opal Tometi as a response to the racism against African Americans found throughout American society as well as its political and social movements. Some have asked to borrow the movement's name and change it to "Our Lives" or "All Lives." Garza argues against this change, saying the movement has a specific aim that could be diluted by widening its scope:

> We're not saying Black lives are more important than other lives, or that other lives are not criminalized and oppressed in various ways. . . . When you drop 'Black' from the equation of whose lives matter, and then fail to acknowledge it came from somewhere, you further a legacy of erasing Black lives and Black contributions . . . we are asking you . . . to stand with us in affirming Black lives. . . . Please do not change the conversation by talking about how your life matters, too. It does, but we need less watered down unity and more active solidarities with us, Black people, unwaveringly, in defense of our humanity. Our collective futures depend on it.[11]

Patrisse Cullors, *second from left*, cofounded the Black Lives Matter movement.

people worldwide were using this hashtag to express their own outrage.

Under the guidance of Cullors and two friends, Black Lives Matter became an international organization. By early 2015, it had chapters in the United States, Canada, and Ghana. It worked to end police killings and change laws to bring equal rights to people regardless of race, sex, or immigration status. The death of Martin and the acquittal of Zimmerman pushed these people into action. Through rallies, social media, and public statements, the activists behind Black Lives Matter and other people around the country spoke out on issues of discrimination and racial profiling.

FROM THE
HEADLINES

ERIC GARNER

On July 17, 2014, a New York City police officer approached Eric Garner. The police had repeatedly arrested Garner for selling individual cigarettes, a minor crime. Before July 17, Garner filed a complaint that an officer had conducted an invasive body cavity search on the street; Garner had plans to press charges.

On this day, he told the police to leave him alone, saying he was not doing anything wrong. Garner had just broken up a street fight, which might have attracted police attention. Four officers wrestled Garner to the ground. One of them, Daniel Pantaleo, held Garner in a choke hold.

The officers cuffed Garner and let go of him, but Garner repeatedly said he could not breathe. Eventually, he lay still until the ambulance crew arrived. They placed him in the ambulance.

At the hospital one hour later, he was pronounced dead. The medical examiner stated his death was a homicide. Although Garner's weight and asthma were contributing factors, the compression of Garner's neck and chest and his position on the ground for a long period of time led to his death.

Still, on December 3, 2014, the grand jury decided no charges would be filed. Protesters marched in New York and across the country. They chanted, "Black lives matter." People were tired of African-American deaths being ignored by the justice system.

Many professional athletes, including basketball star LeBron James, wore "I Can't Breathe" shirts to draw attention to the death of Eric Garner.

PROTECTION

Ferguson is a city with a population that is 67 percent African-American. But out of the 53 officers on the force at the time of the Michael Brown shooting, only three were black.[1] Ferguson is not the only US city with this racial gap between police and citizens. This racial divide has become especially controversial when paired with the increasing militarization of US police forces. The use of military-style weapons and tactics against US citizens has attracted widespread criticism.

Police use of large armored vehicles has drawn criticism from those who believe military-style weapons and tactics alienate police from their communities.

FEAR FROM WATTS

The Watts riots contributed to the militarization of the police not only by changing how police were trained but also through the fear they caused. For five nights, millions of people across the United States watched the riots on television. They watched rioters burn and loot neighborhoods. As they watched, many came to fear potential future riots and looked to the police to keep them safe through whatever means were necessary.

THE WATTS RIOTS AND SWAT

Researchers trace military tactics and gear upgrades back to the Watts riots of 1965, which took place in Los Angeles, California. Following the arrest of an African-American man for suspected drunk driving, a roadside confrontation ballooned into a full-scale riot. During the six days the riots lasted, the police dodged thrown objects, including knives and Molotov cocktails, as well as gunfire from the windows of upper-story apartments. The police were not trained to handle these intense situations. Hundreds of people were injured in the riots, and 34 died.[2]

SWAT teams often use military-style equipment.

When Los Angeles Inspector Darryl Gates noted
his officers in the Los Angeles police force did not have
the training or the gear needed to deal with the riot, he
consulted with the US military. Using what he learned in
these discussions, Gates did something that would change
policing throughout the United States. He started the
first Special Weapons and Tactics (SWAT) unit, a police
force that used military-grade weapons to carry out
high-risk missions.

MILITARY MIGHT

When news anchors discuss police militarization, they
most often focus on the purchase of surplus military
supplies through the 1033 Program, launched in 1997. This
program transfers equipment from the US Department of
Defense to local police forces. By 2005, the organization
that operates the program, the Defense Logistics Agency,
had processed orders for 17,000 US police departments.[4]
These orders included everything from Black Hawk
helicopters and remote-controlled aircraft to M-16 rifles,
grenade launchers, and night vision goggles.

The use of SWAT teams to serve warrants has been criticized for increasing the chances of violent police encounters.

In addition to military weapons, police often employ military tactics. SWAT teams are designed to tackle problems ordinary police cannot, such as intense shootouts or hostage rescue missions. But in some areas, SWAT teams are used to serve warrants and deal with minor arrests. SWAT leaders push for this so teams can actively train.

As a result, police often enter interactions with the public with a high expectation for violence. Critics believe officers sometimes behave more like soldiers in a hostile area than protectors of local citizens, demanding immediate obedience and reacting strongly when it is not forthcoming.

The use of SWAT forces has been disproportionately targeted at people of color, including African Americans. The American Civil Liberties Union (ACLU), an organization that monitors civil rights issues, found 42 percent of the people affected by the use of SWAT teams to execute search warrants were African Americans.[5] African Americans make up approximately 13 percent of the US population.[6]

"PEOPLE WHO THINK YOU COULD WAVE A MAGIC WAND, AND THE LEGACY OF THE PAST IS OVER, ARE BLIND."[7]

—RUTH BADER GINSBURG, US SUPREME COURT JUSTICE, SPEAKING ABOUT RACE RELATIONS

US VERSUS THEM

Some people may take media portrayals of African-American men and boys as frequent criminals at face value. In cases of police shootings, they may question the innocence of the victim. Some might assume these shootings happened because the person who got shot did something wrong, perhaps even violent. On the other hand, some people believe just the opposite. Harassment and degrading interactions with the police have driven them to believe everything negative they hear about the police. Misinformation on both sides of the issue is widely spread through the mainstream media.

Activists hoping for black lives to be treated as equal are calling for significant changes to modern policing practices. Many argue the militarization of police forces contributes to the sense that police are hostile to residents rather than helpful. This distrust between officers and citizens can go in both directions, worsening the problem.

LIMITED VIEW

In 2011, the Pew Research Center conducted a study in which it tracked news outlets in Pittsburgh, Pennsylvania, to see how they represented African-American men and boys. All of these outlets were mainstream, limited to the primary television networks and newspapers. Pew researchers examined almost 5,000 stories and discovered fewer than 4 percent featured a black male who was not either an athlete or associated with a crime.[8]

Traditionally, when mainstream media reports criminal activity, the only facts included are those given to the reporters by the police. This is the case even when the story involves the police shooting of a suspect. The media coverage of the Michael Brown case was unusual in that reporters spoke to people who claimed to be witnesses.

CHAPTER SEVEN

RENISHA
MCBRIDE

S hortly before 1:00 a.m. on November 2, 2013, police in Detroit, Michigan, received a 911 call saying a woman had been speeding down the street and struck a parked car with her own car. Before phoning 911, caller Carmen Beasley spoke to the driver, Renisha McBride. McBride held her head in her hands and told Beasley she could not find her phone. She seemed "discombobulated," Beasley said.[1] While Beasley was making the call, McBride walked away, leaving the scene of the accident.

Because no injuries were reported, the call was a low police priority. Officers did not arrive on the scene until they received a second call. In this call, they were

The killing of Renisha McBride highlighted the risks African Americans face in the United States, even when simply looking for help in an unfamiliar neighborhood.

CELEBRATING THE LIFE OF

Renisha Marie McBride

SUNRISE: APRIL 11, 1994 - SUNSET: NOVEMBER 2, 2013

Service to be held
Friday, November 8, 2013
10:30 A.M. Family Hour • 11:00 A.M. Home Going

House of Prayer and Praise
16520 Wyoming • Detroit, Michigan 48221

told the driver had returned. By the time police got to the scene of the accident, 40 minutes after it originally occurred, the driver had once again left the area.

THEODORE WAFER'S HOUSE

Six blocks from the scene of the accident, a white man named Theodore Wafer had fallen asleep while watching television. He later awoke to banging on the side door and then the front door of his home. He could not find his cell phone, but he turned off the light and the television to hide the fact he was at home.

He looked out the peephole in the front door and saw a figure leaving the porch and heading toward the side door. This time, the banging on the door was hard enough to rattle a window. Wafer later said he thought several people were trying to break into his home. He reached for his shotgun. Wafer returned to the front door. He opened it, saw a person in the dark, and fired. At approximately 4:40 a.m., Renisha McBride lay dead on the porch in front of Wafer's home. She had been shot in the face.

No one knows what happened between the time of the accident and McBride's arrival at Wafer's home.

Days after McBride's death, people held a candlelight vigil at the scene of the shooting.

Her family believed she was hurt, confused, and looking for help. No one came forward who had seen or spoken to her during this interval.

A RACIALLY MOTIVATED CRIME?

As protests sprang up around Detroit, McBride's killing received widespread media attention. People focused on the fact that another African American had died at the hands of a white shooter. Reactions spread across television news and social media.

Civil rights leaders spoke out about the case. "We are in prayer for the family of Renisha McBride but we are also

MORE TO THE
STORY

TICKING CLOCK

People protest about how long it takes to arrest and try a suspect. They may not realize how much is going on behind the scenes.

First, the police must gather evidence. In the shooting of Renisha McBride, police examined Wafer's door for signs of damage to determine whether anyone had attempted a forced entry. They also examined Wafer's shotgun and McBride's car. They interviewed Carmen Beasley. A coroner performed an autopsy, including a toxicology screening. It may take weeks for labs to fully process these screenings.

Next, the police make an arrest. Because of the evidence police uncovered, the prosecuting attorney's office charged Wafer with second-degree murder and he was arrested. After the jury was selected, the trial began on July 22, 2014. The jurors found Wafer guilty. The judge delivered a sentence of 17 years in prison, many months after the shooting occurred.

urgently calling for justice for the loss of this daughter, sister, and friend," said activist Al Sharpton in a statement issued by the Michigan Chapter of the National Action Network.[2]

Sharpton and other activists called for an investigation of the incident. They felt McBride had been profiled and gunned down because she was African-American. They believed the prosecutor's office needed to take action.

As various people pushed the police to make an arrest, the prosecutor's office said it could not make a decision until it had more information from the police department. According to the prosecutor, race played no part in the investigation. In mid-November, the prosecuting attorney's office announced Wafer would be charged with second-degree murder.

MCBRIDE'S BEHAVIOR AND PAST

The medical examiner conducted a toxicology screening after McBride was killed. The results showed she was legally intoxicated, or drunk, and had been smoking marijuana before she hit the parked car.

Wafer's attorneys argued McBride's behavior was a factor in the case and should be revealed to the jurors. They said McBride had sold drugs. They also wanted jurors to know her Twitter account name since it included the word "thuggin." The opposition believed this information had no place in the trial and was irrelevant to the facts of the case.

Wafer testified in his own defense during the trial.

THE TRIAL

When the case went to trial, witnesses detailed the events leading up to McBride's death for the jury. Facts came out about McBride's alcohol consumption before the accident. She and her best friend had consumed vodka and smoked three marijuana cigarettes.

Wafer's defense stressed the fact he believed his home was being invaded. Wafer said he feared for his life. Michigan law includes the so-called castle doctrine. This means a person at home can legally use deadly force instead of retreating if he or she feels threatened. However, the jury rejected Wafer's self-defense claims. The judge in the case, Dana M. Hathaway, said she did not believe race was relevant to the case. She said she thought Wafer had acted out of fear, but added that fear was not an excuse for killing someone. At the end of the trial, Wafer was convicted of second-degree murder. He was sentenced to 17 years in prison.[3]

Though Hathaway thought race was irrelevant to the case, Wafer's defense attorney, Cheryl Carpenter, said she believed the trial had been impacted by other shootings of unarmed African Americans: "I think a lot of people thought in this case that there have been so many unjustified killings of African Americans that do go unnoticed—this could have been Trayvon Martin in our courtroom."[4] The nationwide outrage over the cases of Martin and other victims had made the ideals behind Black Lives Matter an important part of future cases involving the shooting of unarmed African Americans.

ONLINE ACTIVISM

The story of Renisha McBride received significant attention on social media. Between November 6, 2013, and December 6, 2013, more than 42,000 tweets discussed the event. Thousands of comments and Facebook posts were written in response to news stories about the shooting.[5] Users expressed outrage over the killing and called for justice in the case.

CALLING FOR
CHANGE

The residents of Ferguson, Missouri, waited months for the results of the US Justice Department's investigations into possible civil rights violations in their city. The announcement finally came on March 4, 2015. Because of the interest in the case, and in the hopes that transparency would curb possible unrest, the entire 102-page report was made public.

The Justice Department found the Ferguson Police Department and court system had a pattern of civil rights violations that destroyed the trust a community should have in its legal system. Police officers stopped drivers without reasonable suspicion, made arrests without cause, and used unreasonable force. All of

US Attorney General Eric Holder spoke on March 4, 2015, about the US Justice Department's investigation.

these things violated the Fourth Amendment to the US Constitution, which says the police cannot search people or take their property without reason.

The Justice Department found Ferguson's courts did not focus on public safety. Minor offenses led to fines that people could not pay. As a result, they had to go to jail, losing their jobs and homes in the process. This made life difficult for poor residents, causing them to distrust the legal system. The Justice Department noted African-American residents had to pay more fines than did white residents. They also found certain police officers and court officials were openly racist. This situation violated the Fourteenth Amendment's guarantee of equal protection under the law for all citizens. The Justice Department recommended the police

THE FOURTH AMENDMENT

The Fourth Amendment to the US Constitution reads:

> The right of the people to be secure in their persons, houses, papers, and effects, against unreasonable searches and seizures, shall not be violated, and no warrants shall issue, but upon probable cause, supported by oath or affirmation, and particularly describing the place to be searched, and the persons or things to be seized.[1]

The amendment protects people against random searches by the government and police. It led to laws about search warrants, pat-downs, listening to private phone calls, and other types of surveillance.

and courts reemphasize public safety rather than revenue-generating fees. It also called for improved training and police oversight.

The need for more effective policing is not limited to Ferguson. In December 2014, President Barack Obama created the Task Force on Twenty-First Century Policing. One of the goals of the task force is to help police departments build strong relationships with the communities they serve. To do this, the Task Force recommends police departments be transparent, meaning they keep the community informed during investigations and wear body cameras to record their interactions with citizens. Community members should also be able to review police conduct and procedures and make recommendations.

DID DARREN WILSON VIOLATE MICHAEL BROWN'S CIVIL RIGHTS?

To charge Wilson with violating Brown's civil rights, federal laws demand that the government show Wilson used unreasonable force against Brown and that he knew he was doing wrong. The Justice Department reviewed all of the evidence gathered for the criminal case and conducted additional interviews. The Justice Department did not charge Wilson.

Part of the reason is that no solid evidence contradicted Wilson's testimony. His statement is consistent with the physical evidence and the findings of three different autopsies. Early in the investigation, several eyewitnesses contradicted Wilson. These witnesses either disagreed with the physical evidence or later changed their stories. Without solid evidence to challenge Wilson, no charges could be filed.

PROTESTS CONTINUE

Even while local governments work to create community police forces, protests continue. On December 20, 2014, Black Lives Matter staged a series of die-ins across the country. Protesters, sprawled on the floor as if shot, filled public spaces. These protests echoed the sit-ins of the 1960s, when African-American activists sat at whites-only lunch counters and waited to be served. Both forms of peaceful protest brought the protesters' message into public locations where it could not be easily ignored.

In one die-in, protesters filled the central area of the Mall of America in Bloomington, Minnesota, shutting down parts of that shopping center on one of the busiest shopping days

EQUALITY FOR ALL

The civil rights leaders in the 1950s and 1960s, including Martin Luther King Jr. and Malcolm X, were men. In contrast, many of today's leaders, including the founders of Black Lives Matter, are women. Part of their goal is to remake the movement to include groups that often remained marginalized in the 1960s, including women, the disabled, and undocumented immigrants, as well as those who suffer discrimination as a result of their gender identity or sexual orientation. The goal of the movement is not simply to improve life for one segment of the African-American community, but for the community as a whole.

Similar to King, today's leaders are promoting peaceful protest, but also like him, they are promoting active protests that cannot be easily ignored. Modern activists seek to broaden this message to include more people than ever before.

Protesters held demonstrations known as die-ins to bring attention to their message.

of the year. Die-ins were also held at King of Prussia Mall in Philadelphia, Pennsylvania; Towson Mall in Baltimore, Maryland; and Park City Center in Lancaster, Pennsylvania.

On March 6, 2015, police in Madison, Wisconsin, received a call about a fight and a young man jumping out in front of cars. They even had a name—Tony Robinson.

Officer Matt Kenny heard what sounded like a fight within the duplex and forced his way into the home, where he claimed Robinson assaulted him. Kenny then shot and killed Robinson, who was unarmed.

Protests began almost immediately. On March 9, students at the local high school staged a walk-out. They chanted, "We are Tony Robinson. Black lives matter." and "No justice. No peace. No racist police."[2] Another group of protesters filled the Wisconsin

A CONTINUING EFFORT

The efforts of Black Lives Matter continued in the summer of 2015, when several incidents highlighted the vulnerability of African-American lives. The most shocking was the June 17 shooting of ten African-American worshipers at a church in Charleston, South Carolina. Nine of the victims died. The shooter was a white supremacist who had frequently been photographed with the Confederate flag.

In July, the movement drew attention to the death of Sandra Bland in Texas. After being arrested following a minor traffic violation, Bland was found dead in her jail cell. The authorities said she had committed suicide, but protesters disputed this. On July 19, Samuel DuBose was shot by a university police officer in Cincinnati, Ohio, during a traffic stop.

state capitol building, chanting "Indict, convict, send those killer cops to jail—the whole damn system is guilty as hell."[3] Madison's mayor praised the protesters for keeping their events peaceful.

BALTIMORE

An incident in Baltimore sparked some of the most passionate outrage yet over the mistreatment of African Americans by police officers. On the morning of April 12, 2015, police officers stopped and arrested Freddie Gray, a 25-year-old African-American man, in the city of Baltimore. Gray surrendered voluntarily, and the police did not use force to detain him. At 8:42 a.m., officers put in a request for a police van to bring Gray to the station.

PROTESTERS AND RIOTERS

After receiving the US Justice Department's report, Ferguson's mayor announced the police chief was resigning. One hundred and fifty protesters gathered in front of the police station. Despite the presence of police in riot gear, everything remained peaceful until approximately midnight.

That was when someone shot and injured two officers. When a suspect was arrested, District Attorney Robert McCulloch described him as a protester. Protest organizer Bishop Derrick Robinson objected. "I asked him why would he say that he was a protester because it makes us look bad," Robinson said. "It sets us like five steps back to say that it was a protester who did it, but he admitted to me that he'd never protested."[4] Police and newspapers often use "rioter" and "protester" interchangeably, despite the fact that most protests are nonviolent.

MORE TO THE
STORY

BLACK WOMEN AND GIRLS MATTER

Many initiatives, such as President Obama's My Brother's Keeper program, focus on African-American boys. They do so because African-American boys are suspended three times more often than their white peers. African-American girls are six times more likely to be suspended than white girls.[5] Yet there are relatively few girl-oriented programs.

Several groups, including the National Women's Law Center and the African-American Policy Forum, have conducted studies that challenge single-gender programs that remove girls and women from the picture. Their research shows educators often focus more on how African-American female students behave rather than on what they are learning. These organizations are urging President Obama to include African-American girls and women in his initiative.

The African-American Policy Forum focuses on women with its Say Her Name movement, which deals with police brutality against African-American women. The group argues that police killings of African-American men and boys garner major media attention, while similar incidents involving African-American women and girls are largely ignored. Say Her Name is meant to shed light on these incidents in an effort to bring equal justice to all portions of the African-American community.

By 8:46, Gray was in the van. When he arrived at the police station at 9:26, he was having severe medical problems. An ambulance was called and brought him to a nearby hospital. There, he underwent surgery on his spine and fell into a coma. On April 18, protests began at a Baltimore police station. Protesters accused the arresting officers of harming Gray while he was being transported in the van. At 7:00 a.m. on April 19, Gray died at the hospital.

The next day, protests expanded to the police headquarters and Baltimore city hall. At a news conference, police revealed Gray had asked for medical care during his arrest but did not get it. Nonviolent protests continued for the next several days. On April 25, some protesters became violent, damaging police cars and businesses. Gray's twin sister called for an end to the violence, but on April 27, the day of Gray's funeral, major riots broke out in Baltimore.

In response to the riots, Maryland Governor Larry Hogan declared a state of emergency. He called in the National Guard to help quell the riots, and local police forces requested thousands of reinforcements from other states. On April 28, the Baltimore Orioles played a baseball game in an empty stadium due to security concerns. The violence began to settle down, but the calls for justice continued. On May 1, six Baltimore police officers were charged for Gray's death.[6] Some were charged with assault, while others were charged with second-degree murder.

People concerned with unequal treatment of African Americans by police officers watched the case closely as

Members of the National Guard patrolled Baltimore after the onset of rioting.

it developed. Unlike earlier cases, including the deaths of Michael Brown and Oscar Grant, Freddie Gray's death led to quick charges against the officers involved.

Across the country, activists who agreed with the message of the Black Lives Matter movement continued to march and push for improvements in their local police forces and court systems. They demanded justice for Michael Brown, Oscar Grant, Trayvon Martin, Renisha McBride, and the many other people who had lost their lives. They sought to fully root out racism and discriminatory practices. The charges in Freddie Gray's death suggested some of these changes were beginning to take place.

"THERE'S BEEN A SIGNIFICANT AMOUNT OF CONSCIOUSNESS-RAISING THROUGHOUT THE ENTIRE COUNTRY, AND SPECIFICALLY IN MORE MIDDLE-CLASS COMMUNITIES. WHAT HAS BEEN INTERESTING IS THAT MIDDLE-CLASS BLACK FOLK, WHO BEFORE HADN'T IDENTIFIED WITH POOR BLACK COMMUNITIES, HAVE HAD THEIR OWN REVELATIONS."[7]

—PATRISSE CULLORS, COFOUNDER OF BLACK LIVES MATTER

ESSENTIAL
FACTS

MAJOR EVENTS

- In 2012, Alicia Garza creates #BlackLivesMatter with Patrisse Cullors and Opal Tometi.

- In 2014, the Justice Department investigation into the Ferguson Police Department calls for changes in both the police department and the court system, both of which had created a culture of mistrust between city government and the city's black population.

- In April 2015, protests and riots break out in Baltimore following the death of Freddie Gray after his arrest. In May, charges are filed against the officers involved.

KEY PLAYERS

- Oscar Grant is shot and killed in 2009 following a fight on a commuter train; the shooter, an officer who claimed he meant to draw his Taser, is convicted.

- Trayvon Martin is on his way home from a convenience store in 2012 when he is shot and killed by a neighborhood watch member who says he felt threatened by the unarmed teen.

- Renisha McBride is shot and killed in 2013 when a man thinks she is breaking into his home; her killer is convicted.

- Michael Brown is shot and killed in 2014 following a brief struggle with a police officer who says Brown tried to take his gun.

IMPACT ON SOCIETY

In the Black Lives Matter movement, activists raise public awareness through marches and other forms of protest, such as the die-ins that echo the sit-ins of the 1960s. Social media, including Facebook, Twitter, and other online tools, have given people a chance to express outrage and support about these issues. The efforts of activists in the Black Lives Matter movement are bringing issues of unequal police treatment into the public consciousness.

QUOTE

"People who think you could wave a magic wand, and the legacy of the past is over, are blind."

—Ruth Bader Ginsburg, US Supreme Court Justice

GLOSSARY

ACQUIT
To legally say someone is not guilty.

ADVOCATE
To speak or write in support of someone else.

ATTORNEY GENERAL
The main legal adviser to a state governor or the federal government.

AUTOPSY
The examination of a body after death.

CORONER
An official who investigates the cause of suspicious deaths, medically and scientifically examining the body and other evidence.

DELIBERATING
Thinking about or discussing a situation or case before making a decision.

DIVERSITY

The quality of being varied or not all the same.

INDICT

To legally charge someone with a crime.

INTOXICATED

Physically affected by alcohol or other drugs.

JIM CROW LAWS

Laws that segregated or discriminated against people based on race.

JURISDICTION

An area over which a person or group has legal responsibility.

PROSECUTING ATTORNEY

The head lawyer within a county whose job includes trying people for criminal and civil crimes.

TOXICOLOGY

The study of things that are poisonous or that might otherwise affect a person's behavior.

ADDITIONAL
RESOURCES

SELECTED BIBLIOGRAPHY

Bloom, Lisa. *Suspicion Nation: The Inside Story of the Trayvon Martin Injustice and Why We Continue to Repeat It.* Berkeley, CA: Counter Point, 2014. Print.

Higginbotham, F. Michael. *Ghosts of Jim Crow: Ending Racism in Post-Racial America.* New York: New York UP, 2013. Print.

"Investigation into the Ferguson Police Department." *US Department of Justice, Civil Rights Division.* US Department of Justice, 4 Mar. 2015. Web. 16 June 2015.

FURTHER READINGS

Garbus, Julia, ed. *The Brown v. Board of Education Trial.* Farmington Hills, MI: Greenhaven, 2015. Print.

Pinkney, Andrea Davis. *Hand in Hand: Ten Black Men who Changed America.* New York: Disney/Jump at the Sun, 2012. Print.

WEBSITES

To learn more about Special Reports, visit
booklinks.abdopublishing.com. These links are routinely
monitored and updated to provide the most current
information available.

FOR MORE INFORMATION

For more information on this subject, contact or visit the
following organizations:

ACLU: American Civil Liberties Union
125 Broad Street, Eighteenth Floor
New York, NY 10004
212-549-2500
https://www.aclu.org
The American Civil Liberties Union works to ensure equality, freedom, and
justice in equal measure for all Americans. A big part of this is educating
people about their rights as well as how to defend these rights in court
when necessary.

NAACP: National Association for the Advancement of Colored
People
4805 Mount Hope Drive
Baltimore, MD 21215
410-580-5777
http://www.naacp.org
Founded in 1909, the NAACP is among the oldest organizations working
for equal rights and opportunities for African Americans.

SOURCE
NOTES

CHAPTER 1. MICHAEL BROWN AND FERGUSON

1. Jessica Lussenhop. "Grand Jury Expected to Reconvene Today, Unclear if Proceeds Will Ever Be Public." *Riverfront Times*. Riverfront Times, 24 Nov. 2014. Web. 5 Aug. 2015.

2. "Ferguson, Missouri Grand Jury Decision Announcement." *C-SPAN*. C-SPAN, 24 Nov. 2014. Web. 5 Aug. 2015.

3. Nancy Leong. "Getting the Facts Right about the Ferguson Grand Jury Decision." *The Blog*. Huffington Post Politics, 28 Nov. 2014. Web. 5 Aug. 2015.

4. "We Don't Belong Here." *Economist*. Economist, 29 Nov. 2014. Web. 10 Apr. 2015.

5. Judy Melinek. "You Can't Hurry the Truth." *New Scientist* 223.2984 (30 Aug. 2014): 27. Print.

CHAPTER 2. BLACK LIVES IN AMERICA

1. "Declaration of Independence." *The Charters of Freedom*. National Archives, n.d. Web. 5 Aug. 2015.

2. "Montgomery Bus Boycott." *History Channel*. History Channel, 2015. Web. 5 Aug. 2015.

3. "Biography." *Malcolm X*. The Estate of Malcolm X, 2015. Web. 5 Aug. 2015.

4. "Martin Luther King Jr." *Biography*. Biography, 2015. Web. 5 Aug. 2015.

5. Lyndon B. Johnson. "Remarks upon Signing the Civil Rights Bill." *Miller Center*. Miller Center, n.d. Web. 29 Mar. 2015.

6. "Fair Housing Act of 1968." *History Channel*. History Channel, 2015. Web. 5 Aug. 2015.

7. F. Michael Higginbotham. *Ghosts of Jim Crow: Ending Racism in Post-Racial America*. New York: New York UP, 2013. Print. 144.

CHAPTER 3. OSCAR GRANT

1. Demian Bulwa, Charles Burress, Matthew B. Stannard, and Matthai Kuruvila. "Protests over BART Shooting Turn Violent." *SF Gate*. SF Gate, 8 Jan. 2009. Web. 5 Aug. 2015.

2. "Hundreds Demand Answers, Action in Subway Shooting." *CNN*. CNN, 9 Jan. 2009. Web. 27 Aug. 2015.

3. "Rodney King." *Biography*. Biography, 2015. Web. 5 Aug. 2015.

4. "Los Angeles Riots Fast Facts." *CNN*. CNN, 28 Apr. 2015. Web. 5 Aug. 2015.

5. Aisha Harris. "How Accurate Is *Fruitvale Station?*" *Slate*. Slate, 12 July 2013. Web. 5 Aug. 2015.

6. Paul T. Rosynsky and Chris Metinko. "Mehserle Guilty of Involuntary Manslaughter." *San Jose Mercury News*. San Jose Mercury News, 8 July 2010. Web. 5 Aug. 2015.

7. "Violence in California Police Shooting Trial Verdict." *BBC News*. BBC, 9 July 2010. Web. 5 Aug. 2015.

8. Wanda Johnson. "Oscar Grant's Mother: We Have to Be Relentless in the Vindication of Our Slain Sons." *Time*. Time, 26 Aug. 2014. Web. 30 Mar. 2015.

CHAPTER 4. UNEQUAL JUSTICE

1. Joseph Shapiro. "In Ferguson, Court Fines and Fees Fuel Anger." *NPR*. NPR, 25 Aug. 2014. Web. 5 Aug. 2015.

2. Ibid.

3. F. Michael Higginbotham. *Ghosts of Jim Crow: Ending Racism in Post-Racial America*. New York: New York UP, 2013. Print. 157.

4. Christopher Ingraham. "You Really Can Get Pulled Over for Driving While Black, Federal Statistics Show." *Washington Post*. Washington Post, 9 Sept. 2013. Web. 13 May 2015.

5. F. Michael Higginbotham. *Ghosts of Jim Crow: Ending Racism in Post-Racial America*. New York: New York UP, 2013. Print. 158.

6. Paul Butler. "One Hundred Years of Race and Crime." *Journal of Criminal Law and Criminology* 100.3 (Summer 2010): 1047. Print.

7. Ibid. 1048.

8. F. Michael Higginbotham. *Ghosts of Jim Crow: Ending Racism in Post-Racial America*. New York: New York UP, 2013. Print. 157.

9. Richard Thompson Ford. *Rights Gone Wrong*. New York: Farrar Straus Giroux, 2011. 236.

CHAPTER 5. TRAYVON MARTIN

1. Austin Sarat, ed. *Knowing the Suffering of Others: Legal Perspectives on Pain and Its Meanings*. Tuscaloosa, AL: U of Alabama P, 2014. *Project MUSE*. Web. 203.

2. Sudeep Reddy and Neil King Jr. "Top Five Quotes on the Trayvon Martin Case." *Wall Street Journal*. Wall Street Journal, 21 July 2013. Web. 6 Apr. 2015.

SOURCE NOTES
CONTINUED

3. Deepti Hajela. "Trayvon Martin 'Million Hoodie March' March Draws Hundreds in New York City." *Huffington Post*. Huffington Post, 21 Mar. 2012. Web. 5 Aug. 2015.

4. Ibid.

5. Tracy Martin and Sybrina Fulton. "Prosecute the Killer of Our Son, 17-Year-Old Trayvon Martin." *Change.org*. Change.org, n.d. Web. 5 Aug. 2015.

6. Sarah Gonzalez. "Students at 34 Miami Schools Walk Out of Class for Trayvon Martin." *NPR*. NPR, 24 Mar. 2012. Web. 18 Mar. 2015.

7. Anthony Man. "Alcee Hastings Calls for Repeal of Stand-Your-Ground Law." *Sun Sentinel*. Sun Sentinel, 22 Mar. 2012. Web. 5 Aug. 2015.

8. Eric Holder. "Attorney General Eric Holder Addresses the NAACP Annual Conference." *US Department of Justice*. US Department of Justice, 16 July 2013. Web. 5 Aug. 2015.

9. Jon Cohen. "Zimmerman Verdict: 86 percent of African Americans Disapprove." *Washington Post*. Washington Post, 22 July 2013. Web. 5 Aug. 2015.

10. Mark Jurkowitz and Nancy Vogt. "On Twitter: Anger Greets the Zimmerman Verdict." *Pew Research Center*. Pew Research Center, 17 July 2013. Web. 5 Aug. 2015.

11. Alicia Garza. "A Herstory of the #BlackLivesMatter Movement." *Feminist Wire*. Feminist Wire, 7 Oct. 2014. Web. 24 May 2015.

CHAPTER 6. POLICE PROTECTION

1. Wesley Lowery, Carol D. Leonnig, and Mark Berman. "Even before Michael Brown's Slaying in Ferguson, Racial Questions Hung over Police." *Washington Post*. Washington Post, 13 Aug. 2014. Web. 5 Aug. 2015.

2. "Watts Riots." *PBS*. PBS, 2002. Web. 5 Aug. 2015.

3. Jeremy Ashkenas and Haeyoun Park. "The Race Gap in America's Police Departments." *New York Times*. New York Times, 8 Apr. 2015. Web. 13 May 2015.

4. Radley Balko. *Rise of the Warrior Cop: The Militarization of America's Police Forces*. New York: Public Affairs. Print. 209–210.

5. "War Comes Home." *ACLU*. ACLU, June 2014. Web. 5 Aug. 2015.

6. "QuickFacts." *US Census*. US Census, 8 June 2015. Web. 5 Aug. 2015.

7. Sabrina Rojas Weiss. "HBD, RBG! Celebrate with Justice Ginsburg's Most Notorious Quotes." *Refinery 29*. Refinery 29, 15 Mar. 2015. Web. 2 Apr. 2015.

8. Jeannette Wicks-Lim. "Why We *All* Need Affirmative Action." *Dollars & Sense*. Dollars & Sense, November/December 2014. Web. 5 Aug. 2015.

CHAPTER 7. RENISHA MCBRIDE

1. "Renisha McBride was 'Discombobulated' before Theodore Wafer Shot Her: Witness." *NY Daily News*. NY Daily News, 18 Dec. 2013. Web. 5 Aug. 2015.

2. Khalil AlHajal. "Al Sharpton Speaks Up on Renisha McBride Slaying." *MLive*. MLive, 8 Nov. 2012. Web. 1 Apr. 2015.

3. Adam Howard. "Theodore Wafer Found Guilty in Killing of Renisha McBride." *MSNBC*. MSNBC, 7 Aug. 2014. Web. 1 Apr. 2015.

4. Alana Semuels. "Detroit-Area Man Gets 17 to 32 Years for Shooting Visitor on Porch." *Los Angeles Times*. Los Angeles Times, 3 Sept. 2014. Web. 5 Aug. 2015.

5. Tara L. Conley. "Tracing the Impact of Online Activism in the Renisha McBride Case." *MediaMakeChange*. MediaMakeChange, 16 Dec. 2013. Web. 26 Mar. 2015.

CHAPTER 8. CALLING FOR CHANGE

1. "Fourth Amendment." *US Constitution*. Cornell University Law School, n.d. Web. 10 Apr. 2015.

2. "Madison Police Have Shut Down East Washington." *NBC 15*. AP, 10 Mar. 2015. Web. 5 Aug. 2015.

3. Ibid.

4. Eliott C. McLaughlin. "Ferguson Police: Public Info Led to Arrest of Man in Shootings of Two Officers." *CNN*. CNN, 15 Mar. 2015. Web. 5 Aug. 2015.

5. Melinda D. Anderson. "Black Girls Should Matter, Too." *Atlantic*. Atlantic, 11 May 2015. Web. 5 Aug. 2015.

6. "Timeline: The Freddie Gray Investigation." *Baltimore Sun*. Baltimore Sun, n.d. Web. 5 Aug. 2015.

7. Michael Segalov. "We Spoke to the Activist behind #BlackLivesMatter about Racism in Britain and America." *Vice UK*. Vice UK, 2 Feb. 2015. 18 Mar. 2015.

INDEX

ABOUT THE
AUTHORS

Sue Bradford Edwards writes nonfiction for children and teens, working from her home in Saint Louis, Missouri. She studied archaeology and history in college. Her writing covers a range of topics including history and science.

Duchess Harris, JD, PhD, is the author of two books, *Black Feminist Politics from Kennedy to Clinton/Obama* (Palgrave Macmillan) and an edited volume with Bruce Baum, *Racially Writing the Republic: Racists, Race Rebels, and Transformations of American Identity* (Duke University Press). She is a professor and chair of the American Studies Department at Macalester College in Saint Paul, Minnesota.